I0540023

NALEVATE

Spinal Cord Injury Survivor:
Turning Trauma Into Triumph.

NALEVATE

/năl·ə·vāt/   *verb.*

To overcome adversity, and challenges.
Transition, and grow mentally to be the
best version of oneself.

NALEVATE

Published By Books to Hooks Publishing, LLC.

Copyright 2024 © Lanale Robinson

All rights reserved

No part of this book may be reproduced, distributed, emailed, or transmitted in any form or by any means, including photocopying, recording, emailing, or other electronic or mechanical methods, without the prior written consent of the copyright publisher/author, except by a reviewer who may quote passages in a review.

All images, logos, quotes, and trademarks included in this book are subject to use according to trademark, and copyright laws.

All rights reserved. No part of this book may be reproduced in any form or by an electronic or mechanical means, including storage, and retrieval systems, without written permission from the author or publisher, except as permitted by the copyright law or by a reviewer who may quote brief passages in a review.

LANALE ROBINSON
NALEVATE
ROBINSON LANALE

All rights reserved By Lanale Robinson

Printed In the United States of America

FOREWORD

I have had the privilege of witnessing firsthand the extraordinary journey of Lanale. A remarkable individual who has defied the odds, and inspired countless others with his unwavering resilience, and determination.

When I first met Lanale just three months after his devastating injury, his prognosis was uncertain; diagnosed a quadriplegic paralyzed from the neck down. Despite the challenges he faced his spirit remained unbroken, and his resolve to walk again was unwavering. As his therapist, I was humbled by his courage and motivated to match his enthusiasm with challenging yet achievable goals.

Throughout his rehabilitation Lanale consistently demonstrated a growth mindset, pushing past perceived limitations, and overcoming obstacles with grit, and perseverance. His ability to reframe setbacks as opportunities for growth and learning was truly remarkable.

One of Lanale's greatest strengths is his capacity to harness the power of positive self-talk, and mindfulness. Even in the face of frustration and discomfort, he would draw upon these inner resources to calm his mind, and refocus his efforts.

It has been an honor to play a part in Lanale's rehabilitation journey. His transformation from a patient with limited mobility to a confident, walking individual is a testament to the human spirit's capacity for growth, adaptation, and triumph.

Lanale's story is a powerful reminder that with unyielding determination, and the right support, even the most daunting challenges can be overcome. I am proud to have witnessed his journey, and to call him an inspiration.

Dr. Rachel Neuenschwander, PT, DPT

CONTENTS

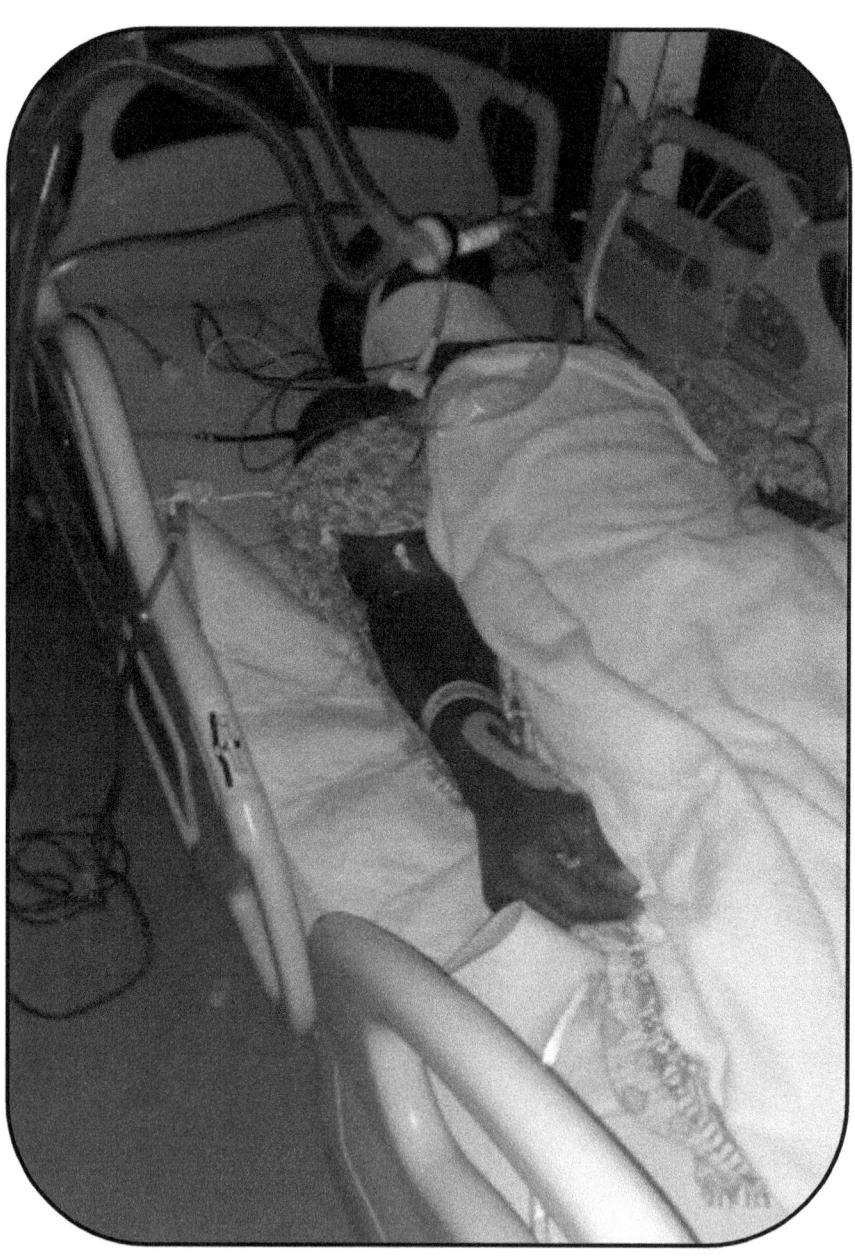

Aultman Hospital

09/12/2021 - 09/21/2021

My journey back to consciousness began with two words. "Mr. Robinson, wake up." The doctor's voice was firm, but reassuring. I slowly opened my eyes. The blurry faces of loved ones, medical staff, and the sterile hospital surroundings came into sharp focus. My doctor's words were simple, and devastating. "Mr. Robinson, you are paralyzed."

On September 12, 2021, while celebrating my thirty-fourth birthday., I encountered a childhood friend, and our interaction escalated into a brief verbal, and physical altercation. With something as simple as an aggressive push, falling over a barrel, and landing on my neck wrong, led me to be paralyzed from the neck down. Diagnosed a quadriplegic incomplete. I damaged my C-5, C-6, C-7. I was told I will never walk again. The weight of my diagnosis was overwhelming. When the doctor spoke those words, my first thought was, what's the next step to get better. My character, positivity, and strength are a few good qualities already instilled in me from my childhood. I'm sure playing sports most of my life, and having a great work ethic helped develop me into the man that I am today.

The doctor went on to discuss certain protocols, and things to expect throughout this recovery. With deliberate attention, I assessed my body's state. Cataloging each sensation, limitation, and symptom with precision. I noticed there was no movement at all. In this unique state, my mind remained fully conscious, and alert. Yet it was entirely severed from its physical counterpart. I'm telling my mind to move my fingers, my toes, or to just even get up. There was no response.

As the doctors, and nurses stepped out of the room, family, and friends started to gather around me. Full of emotion with tears in their eyes, telling me everything's going to be okay. I remained strong. As I lay there, I became increasingly aware of the life-sustaining machinery surrounding me. The intricate network of tubes, and needles attached to my body seemed crucial to my survival. I recall being fixated on these devices, recognizing their vital importance in maintaining my stability.

When I would attempt to speak, I noticed it was hard to swallow my saliva. I was always choking. I had to be suctioned by a tube. This suction procedure had to be done manually. I was fortunate to have a dedicated support system, comprising loved ones, friends, and nursing personnel who collectively ensured my continuous care, and supervision. The surgical procedure involved two strategic incisions. One anteriorly located on the right side of my neck where specialized hardware was implanted. Another posteriorly situated near the spinal cord along the midline of my neck. These carefully executed incisions were crucial to the success of the operation. I was barely able to swallow, or speak effectively.

My doctor would come in my room with suggestions about cutting a hole in my throat, and installing a trek to help airflow to the lungs. Plus, this could help prevent the choking. I then recommended to the doctor to give me a few days to allow my body to heal naturally. This would require someone to be at my bedside twenty-four hours a day. The COVID-19 pandemic has had a profound impact on global health, resulting in significant loss of lives worldwide. At this point, the hospitals only allowed visitors to stay until six pm every day. After that, all guests were required to leave the premises.

The first night of my hospital stay was quite difficult due to the widespread shortage of healthcare professionals, including nurses, and state-tested nursing assistants. I encountered difficulties in obtaining timely assistance despite using the nurse call system. Notably, I encountered repeated delays in receiving care, with average wait times spanning thirty minutes to an hour after initiating a request for aid. Due to the weakened state of my neck muscles, I was unable to vocalize for assistance. I used to have to breathe into a tube to alert the staff that I needed help. On occasion, if the tube was not secured right, it would fall off my gown, and would leave me helpless at times.

So, after I survived night one, I spoke with the administration first thing in the morning. Aultman Hospital graciously accommodated my medical needs by allowing a family member to provide around-the-clock support during my recovery. I am grateful for their compassion, and flexibility. My mother stepped up. At this point in my life, I hadn't spoken to her in years. She agreed to take on the responsibility to help with my care after six o'clock when Aultman Hospital stopped allowing visitors to stay on our unit, due to Covid 19 restrictions. The second night went well. I do remember distinctively this particular late night. There was complete silence around the hospital. I looked around; my mother was sleeping. A pivotal moment came when I tried to get out of bed to use the bathroom, only to discover that I couldn't move. The stark contrast between my active mind, and unresponsive body was alarming. As the reality of my paralysis set in, I was overwhelmed with emotion.

The following day, my mother graciously assumed caregiving responsibilities, ensuring my well-being, and safety after six pm as previously arranged. Amidst the challenges, I was surrounded by a supportive network of individuals who readily stepped forward to offer assistance. My mother would push them away. Then when six o'clock arrived, she would not show up, or wouldn't answer phone calls, and so forth. That went on for a few days. Those days of my life were challenging, and frustrating. Especially trying to navigate a life-threatening situation while attempting to maintain organizational control can be an immense struggle. By the third day, I realized that my mother was unable to provide the support I needed, and her unresponsiveness marked a pivotal moment in my journey toward self-reliance.

Aultman Hospital surrounded me with an extraordinary caregiving team, whose selfless dedication, expertise, and kindness profoundly impacted my journey toward healing. They were students, currently going to school to be state tested for nursing assistance, looking to get extra hours, and hands on experience. Aultman Hospital allowed them to sit with me at night, till the next morning shift change to look after me. There was a different person each night, and day. They all offered an amazing perspective, and experience on life. Each individual was extremely helpful, and kept me safe, and smiling, which helped keep my mind at ease in such a challenging time.

One evening, as the hospital grew quiet, my companion, and I passed the time watching X-Men. The movie provided a welcome distraction, and our laughter echoed through the stillness of the night. Creating a moment of unexpected joy during my hospital stay. I was struck by a particular exchange between Magneto, and one of his loyal followers in the film. He said to his warrior, "The power is within you." The power is within you. Magneto's statement was crafted to instill confidence, and inspire his warrior to tap into his latent powers. Leveraging his unique talents to achieve a greater purpose. When I realized this, I started speaking those words into my mind, and out of my mouth. The power is within you, the power is within you.

In a breakthrough moment, I successfully initiated movement in my right ankle. I was stunned. As our eyes met, my companion and I simultaneously grasped the magnitude of the miracle. She looked at me with amazement and said, "Do it again!" So, as I attempted several times, and gained more confidence, this moment of clarity marked a turning point in my life. I realized that by tapping into my inner strength, trusting in a higher power, and adopting a positive mindset, I could overcome any obstacle. With the right support, and determination, I was empowered to transform my challenges into opportunities for growth, and success.

The next morning, I was greeted by two women therapists stating that Aultman Hospital had approved for me to have fifteen-minute therapy sessions a day. Just for stretching, and movement to keep the blood flowing, and muscles loose. I started to explain to the therapist what happened to me the night before. About speaking power into my mind, and getting a reaction from the ankle. They were amazed. Of course, asked me to do it again as they continued to stretch me, and do some quick reflex movements on both sides of my body. The right ankle reacted again. That moment shattered my expectations, and redefined my understanding of what it means to be alive.

Despite the severity of my condition, my hospitalization at Aultman Hospital was relatively short, spanning just nine days. During my nine-day stay at this facility, I received comprehensive briefings from the medical team, including doctors, nurses, and state-tested nursing assistants. This helped me understand my injury, and treatment options. The hospital staff's exceptional care and compassion were complemented by the love, and support of family, and friends, who provided a steady stream of encouragement, and comfort. This collective support played a vital role in my recovery. Providing me with the strength, and resilience to navigate the road ahead.

People would always ask me if I could feel anything. "Can you feel? Can you feel?" It seemed as when I activated that right ankle with movement, a few days after my surgery. If you were to touch me on my right arm, I would be aware, and know you were doing it. Also, if you were to touch me on my right big toe, I could tell you were touching the right big toe. All that could be accomplished with eyes closed. I experienced a profound appreciation for the swift return of sensation, a milestone that marked a significant step forward. Following the injury I suffered from extensive nerve damage, characterized by intense tingling, and numbness. Although I had to tolerate brief periods of excruciating pain, hope remained a constant motivator.

On day six, my doctors, caseworker, and insurance decided to come up with a care plan to discharge me to a fantastic location in Cleveland, Ohio. Cleveland MetroHealth Clinic. A state-of-the-art rehabilitation center specializing in the treatment of spinal cord injuries, traumatic brain injuries, and other complex neurological conditions. Within those few days, I decided to get my mind right. While I developed a personal care plan, and laser focus that would be effective to help my body recover. On day nine, I bid farewell to the team that had supported me throughout my nine-day journey. The arrival of the ambulance crew marked a noticeable shift in the room's atmosphere. The lead paramedic, who claimed over twenty years of experience, displayed a confrontational demeanor toward the staff. Despite his assurances of a safe transfer to the ambulance, his behavior was unsettling. Amidst the chaos, I had expected a certain level of professionalism, and respect for my family, and staff from the ambulance crew. Unfortunately, the driver's demeanor was aggressive from the start. During the transfer from my bed to the gurney, I was moved abruptly, and improperly, landing heavily on my right shoulder. Subsequent medical evaluation at my next destination revealed a torn right pectoral muscle. Confirmed by X-rays, and further treated with a cortisone injection. This incident not only caused me physical harm but also disrupted my scheduled therapy activities. I remained positive, and calm for safe travel to the next destination.

Cleveland MetroHealth Medical Center

09/21/2021 - 10/28/2021

Upon arrival at the Cleveland MetroHealth Medical Center, I was struck by the facility's expansive size. As I was transported to my room, I couldn't help but notice the hospital's exceptional cleanliness, and attention to detail. Additionally, the presence of a dedicated security team provided a sense of reassurance, underscoring the importance of safety within the facility. I also observed that the hospital had strategically grouped patients with similar conditions on the same floor. In my case, I was placed among individuals with spinal cord injuries. This grouping facilitated a sense of community, and understanding. Fortunately, I had the privilege of occupying a room alone. Which not only ensured my privacy, but also played a crucial role in maintaining my mental, and physical well-being. This was particularly important given the rapid spread of COVID-19 at the time. I appreciated the hospital's efforts to minimize the risk of transmission.

Upon settling in, I was greeted by doctors, nurses, caseworkers, and nursing assistants. All had different protocols, procedures, and assessments. The healthcare team developed an individualized care plan to facilitate my recovery, by incorporating targeted interventions, and strategies tailored to my specific needs. The doctors gave me a brief introduction about themselves, and their experience gained from extensive education, training, and clinical studies. The nurses gave me the rundown on my medications on how they will be facilitated throughout the day. Then thoroughly explained the catheterization procedure schedule. Outlining the timing, and frequency of the interventions to ensure optimal care, and minimize complications. Comprehensive skin, and hair assessments were integrated into my care plan to ensure a thorough evaluation of my overall health. My nurse then provided reassurance of their availability twenty-four hours a day to address any questions or concerns that may arise during my care journey. The caseworkers came in to check on my mental health. I'll never forget they would ask the same thing at every location. Sock, blue, bed, you had to repeat those three words back. Case management would use those words to test your memory. I was also asked questions to see how I was handling my injury, and some personal information to help get to know me better.

My initial experience on the first day was overwhelmingly positive. Marked by a sense of professionalism, and expertise. It was evident that the staff possessed specialized knowledge, and skills in caring for patients with quadriplegia, which was reflected in their day-to-day interactions and interventions. Cleveland MetroHealth Hospital serves as a referral center for patients requiring acute rehabilitation providing high-intensity interdisciplinary care. Notably, this location offers an intensive therapy program where patients can receive up to one hour of physical therapy per day as authorized by their insurance provider. Helping patients improve their mobility, and function primarily in the legs, and lower extremities.

In addition to physical therapy, occupational therapy plays a vital role in rehabilitation. Occupational therapy intervention uses everyday life activities to promote health, well-being, and the ability to participate in daily activities. This includes all upper body extremities, especially the hands, and fingers. Speech therapy was a vital aspect of my rehabilitation. Focusing on restoring my ability to communicate effectively, and clearly. Due to the weakening of neck muscles resulting from surgery. At this critical moment, I gained the privilege of having access to new state-of-the-art equipment and collaborating with a team of experienced healthcare professionals.

I reflected on how I could maximize my potential for recovery. My right ankle, and arm had demonstrated mobility, providing a beacon of hope. This glimmer of progress inspired me to explore ways to leverage this momentum in my rehabilitation journey. By combining creative thinking, listening, and a commitment to learning. In that moment of reflection, I recognized that my life had entered a new era of interdependence. The sudden need for assistance with even the most mundane tasks forced me to confront the limits of my independence, and adapt to a new reality. One in which the support of others was essential to my well-being. Learning patience, and meditation. Two very helpful techniques that I knew I would have to master, and use as a tool to help me every day on this challenging journey.

I can remember one evening specifically when the flies were a menace in Ohio. A minor yet unsettling incident occurred when a fly landed on my head. This moment revealed the extent of my vulnerability. In that moment, I was confronted with the limits of my control, and the intensity of my emotional response. Through meditation, I found a means to transcend the discomfort, and access a state of inner calm. This deliberate shift in focus enabled me to rise above the irritation, and reclaim a sense of serenity. I tried Reiki, a holistic therapy that can be used with traditional medical treatment. It's performed by an experienced individual who hovers over you with very light touch that's supposed to help with healing energy. My first experience was a thirty-minute session. The woman turned on some calming music, and began to go on about her routine. I took a few deep breaths closed my eyes, and started to meditate. I was optimistic about the procedure's potential, given its reported success by others. Just after a few minutes go by in my session, I hear the woman packing up her things. She leaves. A little later that evening, an aide came in my room to care for me. I explained to them what happened with the Reiki lady. They laughed, and said the Reiki woman left because she thought I was in a deep sleep. That she would come back later. We laughed so hard. Meditation proved to be highly beneficial.

Patients, I immediately understood by being observant. During my stay I became aware of the significant staffing shortages within the facility, compounded by the COVID-19 pandemic. The delayed response to my nurse call light was a significant concern, and I often wondered if my situation was being prioritized appropriately. However, I recognized that I was not the only patient requiring care. The nursing staff was working diligently to attend to the needs of all patients across the floor, and the facility. Despite the challenges I was impressed by the dedication, and resilience of the nursing staff who worked tirelessly to provide care to all patients, often under difficult circumstances.

Being diagnosed as a quadriplegic with paralysis from the neck down, many might assume that my life was reduced to being bedridden, and stationary. However, losing functional muscle control throughout my body revealed a far more complex reality. In this vulnerable state, I came to understand that I was susceptible to a multitude of secondary complications, and challenges. The respiratory, digestive, nervous, and immune systems are all at risk of disruption, with potentially far-reaching consequences. The intense muscle spasticity, and tone that often accompany quadriplegia, can further compromise these systems increasing the risk of adverse outcomes. Additionally, the skin is prone to breakdown, and complications. While the mental health implications of quadriplegia can be deeply distressing, and have a lasting impact on overall well-being. Through my experiences, I have gained a profound appreciation for the fragility, and resilience of the human body.

The darkest night of my recovery had arrived. With my body immobilized, I faced the ultimate test of my resilience. I recall experiencing a complex cluster of symptoms, including severe right shoulder pain, a torn pectoral muscle, and chronic neck pain. Despite significant nerve damage, I retained partial sensation enabling me to perceive, and respond to these physical discomforts. A jerking motion would pass through my body with intense, deep, aggressive spasticity movements.

It was attacking my stomach, my neck specifically. Some spots felt as if the muscle was going to rip off the bone, or the knots in my stomach were going to explode. The doctors wouldn't be in until morning. The nurses on the floor kept telling me they had given me all the medicines they could for the period, that I would have to wait until my next cycle for something else to ease my discomfort.

Panic set in, fueled by crippling pain, muscle spasms, and a suffocating fear of death. I struggled to breathe. My body felt like it was shutting down. In hopelessness, I clung to a single thought. This will pass. But the pain was overwhelming, leaving me helpless, and consumed by fear. In a desperate moment, I called an individual from my hospital bed. I was unable to hold the phone myself due to my injury. My aide held the phone for me as I shared my darkest fears that I might not survive. My words were filled with panic, and uncertainty. I was lucky to have made it through that terrifying experience. My mind, and body were out of sync, causing confusion, and disorientation. There were times when I would be lying in bed, and I would feel that something was crawling on my left leg. Then when I would start to scratch it, I would notice that the itch would be on the right leg. My nerves were damaged, and were sending false signals everywhere. This was frustrating.

I was catheterized daily every four to six hours. I sought guidance from my doctor regarding the likelihood, and timeline for recovering normal bladder function. My doctor's words stuck with me. Regaining control over your urinary, and bowel functions will be the most challenging part of your recovery. She explained that this process would take time, patience, and rehabilitation. That there were no guarantees of a full recovery. This conversation had a profound impact on me, as I struggled to come to terms with the loss of autonomy, and dignity that accompanied my medical condition. The necessity of catheterization, although medically essential left me feeling vulnerable, and exposed. The frequent need for healthcare professionals to attend to my care, often in the presence of visitors, caused me significant distress. At times, the procedure was accompanied by discomfort, and pain, leaving me feeling humiliated.

Yet, as I navigated this difficult journey, my mindset shifted toward my diet, which I thought would be very important when you think of the digestive system, and what it supports, and provides. The surrounding nerves, muscles, and organs depend on each other as food, and fluids pass through being chemically broken down so they can be absorbed into our bloodstream. The digestive system also helps get rid of waste material. I recognized that the medication, and nerve damage sustained from my injury played a significant role in my inability to urinate independently. Seeking alternative solutions, I began researching the potential benefits of sea moss. A natural product known for its various health advantages. I decided to investigate further, and discovered a high-quality A+ grade sea moss product. Although I cannot attribute my recovery solely to sea moss, I did notice significant improvements after incorporating it into my diet. As I focused intently on recapturing the muscle memory, and mental associations linked to independent urination, I also used the sea moss as directed. Within two weeks, I regained the ability to urinate on my own. The next morning, I shared my progress with my doctor. She examined me, and noted the improvement, but her expression remained neutral. Despite her reserved response, I felt encouraged by my progress. Within two months of surgery, I was able to discontinue catheter use. A significant milestone in my recovery.

Moving forward, I prioritized healthier, eating habits. The head chef was incredible, very professional, and always had a smile on his face.

Even the cooks under him understood the importance of standards in serving quality food. When errors were made in the kitchen, or on the menu, corrections were made immediately. The food at MetroHealth Cleveland Clinic was consistently fresh, hot, and well-presented. We had a variety of options to choose from, and the quality was exceptional.

Next on the list was housekeeping. Though MetroHealth Cleveland Clinic was fully staffed with housekeeping, I was able to have the same housekeeper my whole stay there. This made it easy for a day-to-day routine to be established. She was an older lady who kind of reminded you of your grandma who didn't cut any corners, and was just a hard worker. She cleaned thoroughly, plus understood the standards of organization, and quality work. She took pride, and had tons of passion for her residence, and career. Every day, my room was stocked with fresh towels, washcloths, and gowns, plus other small things that the nurses, and aids might need to assist me throughout the day. My bathroom stayed clean for my visitors. My floors were always swept, and mopped. My cup was always fully stocked in the morning with ice in water. When she was given the chance, and I wasn't in bed, clean sheets, and bedding were provided. I was amazed at how easy she was to talk to. She was pleasant, and soft-spoken. She would come into my room every morning, and realize that my TV was on the same channel for weeks. She would laugh, and then suggest that I could always call for help to change the channel. I then explained to her that growing up as a kid, watching these shows brought me joy.

I watched the episodes of Martin, Fresh Prince, and Jamie Foxx show almost every day. It was on repeat nonstop when I wasn't in my head, or taking care of business for my recovery. Well, let's say, Sundays during football season, that wasn't the case. It seemed that majority of the TVs at Cleveland MetroHealth was on the Cleveland Browns game. The staff were die-hard Cleveland Browns fans. I'll never forget the love, the passion, the screaming in the rooms, or hallways. They would enjoy themselves, win or lose. I can truly say things like this made it much easier for me during my stay at Cleveland MetroHealth.

My nurses were unique in their own way. They had their daily routines, which was effective in getting the job done for their shift. My med pass was pretty heavy at the beginning of my recovery. To start, I was placed on a neurogenic bowel program. I had to take a pill called colace, which is a stool softener. Senna or MiraLAX daily, with sometimes digital stimulation with bisacodyl suppository. Constipation was a constant battle at the beginning of my journey. Midodrine was used to treat low blood pressure as I was always on a constant blood pressure monitor routine. For pain control, they recommended Tylenol for mild pain. Lidocaine patches were used daily for pain management in needed areas. Oxycodone for moderate to severe pain. Gabapentin, baclofen, methocarbam, and tizanidine were all taken for muscle spasms, pain, and nerve damage. Then there was the melatonin to help with sleep, also sometimes Xanax to help with anxiety. I remember I used to have to get an injection called lovenox deep between my abdominal wall to help prevent me from getting blood clots. Bactrim was used for urinary tract infections. There were daily vital capacity checks which was so important. Skin assessments were performed routinely. Weight shifting was required whether I was lying down in bed, or up in a wheelchair. Most of the time, this procedure was performed by an aid.

Without the proper movement, and rotation could result in bedsores which could hinder my recovery in so many ways. So, on day one, I was placed immediately on a two-hour check in change, twenty-four hours every day. This meant every two hours an aide would be responsible for coming in my room to make sure that I didn't need changed. Then they would rotate me in a different position to relieve pressure from certain areas, and do a life check.

There was a particular time I could remember it was my shower day. Now at this point of my recovery, I was only getting bed baths. The aid on hand thought a hot shower would be more therapeutic, and appropriate. My first thought was how they would make me stand up in the shower, and clean me. No way did this sound safe. I just had bad thoughts, imagining so many different scenarios. I couldn't fathom my current health status to be able to handle myself in the shower. So, after I declined a few times, one particular day. She asked me with confidence, and a big smile. Reassuring me everything was going to be ok. I agreed. She then came into my room with this big, comfortable, look-alike lawn chair with massage probes on it that was waterproof, and had wheels. It was perfect. She successfully hoyer lifted me from my bed into my shower chair. Wheeled me into the shower room, and safely cleaned me up thoroughly.

The one-on-one conversations, the extra time spent together with specific individuals will be forever cherished. All in all, the doctors, nurses, and aides at MetroHealth Cleveland Clinic did a phenomenal job. My family and friends continued to come in to see me. From Aultman Hospital to Cleveland MetroHealth Clinic was about a forty-five minute drive. I had a pretty tight core support group. There would be many times family members, or friends would come up to help me with self-care. Like cutting my hair, or grooming my nails, and toes. Making sure my teeth, and skin all remained in good condition. They continued to keep me in the loop on what was going on in the world.

They sat by my bedside days, and nights with comforting words. Words of wisdom, laughter, and joy.

I remember in Cleveland, the food in particular was great. There were so many different cuisines to try. My family, and staff members made sure I tried most of them. From soul food, to Cuban food, to Chinese food, Greek, and Italian. They would provide me with comforting things like pillows, blankets, personal hygiene. I remember that the late-night phone calls were so helpful when I couldn't sleep, or was uncomfortable. The aide, or nurse would have to come into my room, prop a pillow, or a towel up along my shoulder. To place the hospital phone in a position where it wouldn't fall over so that I could hear, and speak on the phone with a little privacy. My team was fully committed to my comfort, and well-being, providing me with everything I needed to recover.

With the groundwork laid, I was ready to begin the rigorous process of rehabilitation, and reclaim my health. My occupational therapy team showed up. According to insurance at this particular location, and time of my recovery, it offered sixty minutes of occupational therapy, sixty minutes of physical therapy. Also including sixty minutes of speech therapy, with all services provided five days a week. They were all supervised, and executed with a care plan in mind. After evaluating me, therapy could help me regain some sort of independence, and mobility for day-to-day living. Why I was sent to an acute intensive therapy location so early, nine days after being paralyzed from the neck down, I was confused. I could only move my right ankle, and arm slightly. My care plan showed that insurance would only cover a short stay at rehab. I knew I had to make the most of the time.

I was assisted by my OT therapist five days a week every morning between seven, and nine o'clock, to either help me with feeding, hygienic needs, dressing, and also stretching. This became a routine for my four to six week stay at MetroHealth rehabilitation clinic. I would have two main occupational therapists on rotation with a trainee. Two therapists with the same passion for the job, with different perspectives, and teaching methods on recovery. They did fantastic. I used machines like the bionic arm which helped facilitate movement in the hands. It's like a robot with attachments that hooked up to a computer, and performed whatever exercise that was programmed for my hand. We did various activities to help regain muscle memory, and upper body parts to be stretched, or strengthened. There were times they would strap me to a motorized arm, and hand therapy machine, to help facilitate rotation, and forward, backward movements with resistance if needed. Though I couldn't wrap my fingers, and hold the handles, the bandages they used secured my hands to stay on.

I continued to progress daily with just the small things. Even with the setbacks going back to the mishandling of the ambulance driver while being transferred from the hospital bed to his transport gurney. I was diagnosed with a torn pectoral. I was limited to right side activities which affected therapy. If I can remember, it limited me to specific exercises for about two to three months of healing time. It also affected my therapy progress notes. I remember having to get x-rays, and cortizone shots to help alleviate the pain, and discomfort. I worked through it all. In the early stages of this recovery, the right side still showed more gains than the left side of the body. After evaluating me, my physical therapist would use exercises to help me move better, starting with stretching, and promoting blood circulation. Muscle and nerve recovery using various equipment, and activities, especially massages.

My therapist would also focus on improving transfers moving from bed to wheelchair. The equipment used was a sliding board, or a ceiling-mounted hoyer lift guided on a track system which was so convenient, and safe. I remember the sliding board transfers used to be so painful, and scary. At this point in my recovery, I felt like my body was a noodle, no control whatsoever. I had to put my full hundred percent trust in my therapist to use her experience, and training techniques to help facilitate me from my wheelchair to my bed. It was challenging. Though I succeeded several times, I felt more comfortable using the hoyer lift machine. They would tell me things like try to stand up or move the right leg, or left arm, shift your weight here. Things that may have seemed far out of reach now in my recovery, but still were obtainable goals with the right mindset. Each of my therapists was very helpful, educational, professional, plus very easy to talk to about how I was feeling.

I remember going into the physical therapy room. It was so big. There were ten tables with hydraulic lifts which were very important for certain activities. I observed the effective use of ceiling-mounted hoyer lifts to transfer patients safely, and efficiently. These lifts were particularly useful in specific situations providing an added layer of support, and stability. The therapists demonstrated a strong commitment to punctuality, and the facility was well-equipped with a wide range of equipment to meet the diverse needs of patients. For the first week or so, I used a regular manual wheelchair which was very uncomfortable, and I didn't feel safe.

My insurance and therapist decided to acquire a Q quantum power electric chair, spending countless hours showing me how to operate it. I was safely secured in with two seatbelts: one at the lower waist, the other seatbelt was supporting the upper trunk to help stabilize me while I was sitting, or operating the wheelchair. I was allowed to customize my wheelchair personally. Obviously, I chose orange, and black as I'm from Massillon. The power chair was amazing; it improved my daily lifestyle. I didn't have to feel so bed-ridden with no freedom. Now I had transportation. It was like my first big step toward independence of my recovery. This chair had a tilt button so you could recline it. You could do different positions for shifts, which is so important to prevent pressure sores. It had a speed gauge on it, a mileage reader. The wheelchair had a bluetooth speaker built into it, lights, a horn. And plenty of power for the outdoors. In the beginning, it took some getting used to. Just due to my fears of being transferred into it by the help of someone else, and not on my own. Plus, the pain I used to suffer after sitting in the wheelchair for fifteen minutes or an hour. The neck pain, the shoulder pain, the dizziness would become noticeably uncomfortable. It took building up some tolerance. Once I had gotten past that stage, my wheelchair was my best friend. My therapist made me do constant wheelchair safety assessments, and test. To make sure my wheelchair would be handled safely at each location, I went around to meet the residents, and staff members. Most importantly, they made sure my wheelchair was comfortable, equipped, and fit to my liking before my discharge to my next location. It worked out perfectly. Now I was rolling.

My speech therapist was special. She helped me with issues for example, like swallowing. The weakness of the muscles in my throat from my surgery were still not healed. Thankfully, early on in my recovery, I was able to eat solid foods. I didn't have any diet restrictions. The last thing I wanted was to have my food blended up altogether in a blender which is called purée. Food which is an alternative meal replacement for people that have swallowing issues. She helped me with social problem-solving, which I thought was so important with me dealing with such a traumatic injury. She was very experienced, easy to open up to.

After doing my evaluation, and assessment, the doctors, and speech therapist were aware, and noticeably understood that I was thinking, and speaking clearly in the right mindset. So they took a different approach with my speech therapy sessions, which included various breathing activities that were effective, and important. I participated in an expiratory muscle strength training program which involved using equipment like a peep valve to blow into. This measures the strength of airflow capacity you were pushing out into the tube. Which gave us a baseline to measure, and keep track of my future improvements. Early on in my recovery, my breathing was very weak, and shallow. It took time to build up. I remember having to use a nebulizer two times a day. This helps release medications into a vapor into my lungs to help relieve some of the issues I was having with my respiratory system. I was equipped with different techniques, and exercises from my speech therapist to incorporate in my day-to-day activities. Breathing exercises, and my meditation worked hand-in-hand.

I really enjoyed the social problem-solving activities. Her challenging techniques, and approach forced me to use my brain in more ways than I could've imagined. I remember my family would come up to visit, and participate in some of the activities with us. It was fun. Though my journey was still just beginning, I was listening, and learning from so many amazingly professional people. I felt that after this place, no place could compare as my days were dwindling, and they were looking for a different place of residence for rehabilitation. I remember the staff used to inform me. That the high-quality care that I received here at their location would drop off tremendously. Every location does not provide, or can maintain the same level of standards, or care that I would expect, and need. To be aware, and ready for changes.

Honestly, at this point of my injury, and where my mindset was, my foundation was solid. I had some information about my injury. My mind was in a healthy confident space, and I had a support team. My body was showing small signs of improvement.

I was approached by a woman coordinator who was in charge of a study, titled psychosocial impact for navigating care transitions on caregivers of people with spinal cord injury. As she began to tell me her involvement with Cleveland MetroHealth Hospital, and with the research study, about how it benefited others in various ways, I agreed to participate. The purpose of the study was for them to ask me specific questions related to my injury to help better understand my mindset on how the injury impacted me. Also, how the injury may have affected the people around me. These are just a few examples. So I would have members in my support team participate. That way, if I was being transitioned back into the community, home, or nursing home, we would know what to expect, and how to care for me safely. Also, the study advisor would provide information to better utilize my resources in the community.

The interviews would provide me with questionnaires about various questions that would last approximately a half an hour, to an hour with only two visits that would occur between a six to twelve month span.

We were compensated ten to twenty-five dollars per session, according to how long the interview took. The funds would be uploaded on a pre-paid visa card that was given to us upon our acceptance in the study. It wasn't much, but it was an appreciated gesture of saying thank you for letting them gather sensitive data from my injury, and my outlook on how I was healing from it. Supporting in participating in their cause that would help many more who were in similar situations who dealt with spinal cord injury trauma, is what raised my awareness. This study was sponsored by a grant from the Craig H Neilsen foundation, which participated in more interviews after doing my research further down the road. I found this study, and staff to be very helpful.

Cleveland MetroHealth employees, and experience, I can say is a huge part of my start to success on this healing journey. Although everything didn't operate always as planned. My caseworker showed up. Even though upon my arrival she, and I would have had a few small conversations about various things. I figured being a caseworker, she would be able to provide me with helpful information about transferring to my next location. Whether that was to a nursing home, or back into the community living with family. Which at this point due to my health, a nursing home was the best option. Then my case worker went on to tell me that my insurance has not yet been approved for my medical bills, or my stay at Aultman Hospital, my previous location. Now, I also have an unpaid balance for medical expenses at my current location, Cleveland MetroHealth. I began to explain to her that my family had taken care of the paperwork when I was at Aultman Hospital, and that it would take some time. Then after doing further research, I found out the paperwork was never submitted. Another setback. So in my mind, I was hoping this wouldn't interact with my transition to my next location.

We worked diligently with job and family services to get my medical insurance expedited, and approved. It still was challenging. I remember calling jobs and family with my case manager present. Explaining to them that I was just diagnosed a quadriplegic. Paralyzed from the neck down, that I can't fill out any paperwork on my own. That I can give consent to either my case manager, or family member to do so to get the paperwork submitted. The woman on the phone must have ignored what I was saying, and asked me if I could just write a letter stating about my injury after I just explained to her that I was paralyzed. Then went on to ask if someone wrote the letter for me if I can still sign my initials. They made the process more complicated than it had to be. With the little bit of patience, persistence, and professionalism, we got it approved.

Now it was time to find my next location. My case manager would come in my room with handfuls of paperwork of nursing homes with different ratings, and in different areas. Just so I could see what my options were to best fit my situation. My family, and I sat down for hours, and days reviewing, and filling out applications, anticipating a smooth transition. After looking over some of the places that we found were suitable, I submitted the list to my case manager. Shortly I discovered all five applications were denied immediately. I was told to find another five locations to resubmit, and try again. So I did. Same results, denied. So now out of ten locations within just a week, I began to get frustrated. I wasn't sure what the problem was.

My case manager then sat down, and explained to me. She had exhausted all options. That my criminal background was the reason, the nursing home administrators denied my application. I was going to have limited options for a long-term, or short term stay in a nursing home system in the state of Ohio. It would take making a few phone calls, and some thorough research to find a location that would accept me. When I was young, I made irresponsible decisions that I took full accountability for. Through my hardship, I was able to grow, and learn from my mistakes to become a better version of myself. Now I lay there, and began to take this information in. Growing up as a kid. I was always aware that when you caught a felony on how it could impact, or jeopardize your employment, or housing arrangements. Also, how the world frowns upon felons, and can be so judgmental of their past. I never would've thought having a criminal background could affect your healthcare. This was a learning moment for me.

I began to think outside of the box. If my ten previous applications got denied by being faxed over, I requested my caseworker if we could do a face-to-face visit with the building case coordinators for the places we were applying for. That if someone from the locations could come, and get to know who I was as a person. Showcase to them my professionalism, my determination to overcome this injury. Even though there were rules, and guidelines within the system to follow. That face-to-face meeting could possibly make all the difference in how much more work a person was willing to put on an individual due to the personal connection. So she began to set up interviews. I spoke with two coordinators about locations that may be suitable for me as time continued to pass. Then she found a nursing home. Edgewood Manor Of Lucasville, in West Virginia. My application was approved. My case manager would go on to say this place specialized in helping recovering quadriplegic, and that this place was equipped with the things I needed for my recovery. That this location would best benefit me, and would be a great experience. At this point, my options were limited. I immediately accepted. Now as Edgewood Manor Of Lucasville, and my case manager were finalizing my paperwork for my transfer, an individual, and I submitted important paperwork pertaining to victims of crime. The Ohio Crime Victims Compensation Program, which is a state government program that provides innocent victims of violent crime, and their families with up to fifty thousand dollars in financial assistance for certain out-of-pocket expenses resulting from a crime. The program is administered by the Ohio Attorney General with Judicial Review provided by the Ohio Court Of Claims. Early on in my recovery, the out-of-pocket expenses were growing.

After taking all steps necessary for filling out paperwork, and dealing with gatekeepers on the phone, to reveal the application was denied. Reason was stated that if the victim has been arrested, or convicted of any felony, or domestic violence, or child endangering offenses within ten years of being victimized, request denied. So again, my past mistakes would play a critical part in such an unrelatable situation. That was now affecting me in so many ways on my healing journey. I remained positive, and calm for safe travels to the next destination.

Edgewood Manor Of Lucasville

10/28/2021 - 11/25/2021

Traveling to my next destination was tough on my body. The roads were rough, with potholes, and constant stopping, and starting. Construction was everywhere, making the ride even bumpier. I wasn't looking forward to the three-and-a-half-hour drive to my third destination. Due to my health condition, regular repositioning was essential to prevent pressure sores, and to keep me as comfortable as possible. I remember there was a driver who was in charge of getting us to our location. Then there was an individual who sat in the back with me to assist with my personal needs. COVID-19 in 2021 seemed to ruin, and affect a lot of things in the workforce worldwide. There was a huge shortage of ambulance drivers at the time. I often heard them vent about their jobs complaining about long hours, low pay, and high stress. They'd also share frustrations about daily life, but occasionally our conversations would turn lighthearted, and enjoyable.

Upon arrival at Edgewood Manor Nursing Home, I was struck by a pungent smell of cigarette smoke in the lobby. Despite being a smoke-free facility, the odor was still overwhelming, and noticeable. We began to get checked in. We did our COVID-19 test. We all passed. I was then taken down a hall with locked doors. Doors that you had to use a PIN code, or key to get into. There were twelve rooms on this hall with two residents per room. I remember asking a staff member why do I see four hallways, and three of them are open for residence to walk around freely. Then our hallway is the only one with the lock on the door. She then explained to me that our particular hallway is for gentlemen with behavior issues, or a criminal background. That raised a red flag for me. Compared to my previous facility, which had an open, and welcoming environment, Edgewood Manor Nursing Home felt restrictive, and isolating. The atmosphere seemed more similar to a secured facility than a nursing home. We could look through the locked door window, and see everyone else roaming around, and interacting with one another. Then the residents in our hall were sheltered until their designated smoke times, or therapy.

Despite my limited mobility, I was concerned about the facility's layout, and operations. The whole setup seemed a bit depressing. Most of us were paying the same for room and board, unless you're private pay. But we didn't have all the same privileges around the facility. Having to live in an environment that is enclosed for long periods of time without something to do can be detrimental to your everyday well-being. When I arrived at this location, I came with the mindset of rehabilitation services. Getting settled into the nursing home was the same procedure at the previous two locations. Doctors, nurses, caseworkers, same protocol, sock, blue, bed. A familiar process that I had done before at this point so it went a lot smoother.

Now that I had my things organized, and put away in my room, I was approached by an individual who didn't appear to be a staff member due to their attire, and personal grooming. Despite their courteous demeanor, I was taken aback by their offer to provide me with food. They mentioned that I had missed lunch at the facility, and suggested that I might want something to eat. Then asked me what I like, and let me know my options. We agreed on a grilled cheese sandwich. The woman returned shortly to let me know that she made my food personally. That she would also sit down, and feed it to me. I was thankful. As the individual began to pick up a piece of the grilled cheese, she sneezed on my food so hard, and was totally aware of it. Then tried to continue to serve me. I denied it immediately. Needless to say, I didn't eat at this location on my first day.

Moving along to day two. I can remember being introduced to some of the new staff members who would be helping me with my care. There was a particular instance when it was time for my rotation, and two-hour check in change. The beds were small. After a few minutes of the two individuals bickering back-and-forth about unrelated work events, also with the look of confusion on their faces on how to assist me. I then started to explain to them that there was a particular way I would like to

31

be handled, and that I could guide them through a routine. The gentleman went on to tell me on how he's done this type of work before, and how I was in good hands. He assured me not to worry. So I was ok with them trying it their way because I understood there's more than one way to get a job done.

 Shortly after they rolled me, my legs hit the floor fast, and hard. They were shocked, and didn't know what to do. I immediately explained to them that I was ok to just help my legs back up on the bed. Let's reposition me, allowing me to show them the system Cleveland MetroHealth staff used to safely position me to get me comfortable. After a thorough review of my body, there were no further injuries or bruising. Only to receive an I'm sorry Mr. Robinson. I was still alarmed as I was looking around very few of the staff wore scrubs, or professional attire. The majority of them wore their regular clothes, even the nurses. There were no name tags, no walkie-talkies for communication.

At Cleveland MetroHealth Rehabilitation Hospital, everyone was equipped with walkie-talkies. The facility understood the importance of communication. Especially in a life, or death situation for a staff member, or a resident's safety. There was a call light button that I had access to in my room. That would signal a blinking light outside above my door that didn't make any noise to alert an employee. If a staff member wasn't in the hallway, residents would have to call out for help, which could result in slower response times. The day shift, I noticed, was equipped with more staff. During the night shift, I would struggle more because administration wouldn't be in the building after five o'clock to supervise. Night shift would completely take advantage of the opportunity.

I remember a particular employee would sit in the lunch room in our hall with his headphones for hours on his shift, without checking on any residents. This was consistent, and disappointing. Considering that some residents on our floor required occasional supervision due to cognitive impairment periods. It was essential to provide adequate support, and monitoring. One particular night, I'll never forget when I hit the help call light. No one came in for over an hour, and I dozed off. Now, once you turn on the call lights at this nursing home, a staff member has to come in your room to physically turn the light off that's located on the wall next to my bed. Now, like I said, my lights had been going off for over an hour when I fell asleep in the middle of the night. I woke up to catch a staff member sneaking into my room, tip toeing, so they wouldn't have to assist me, and to cut the help light off. All I wanted was to be rotated, and my urinal emptied so that it didn't spill over on me while I was sleeping. I was so uncomfortable that night. It was like at this time in the world, nobody was trying to work.

The administration was aware that this type of behavior was happening on several occasions with the employees in the building. Call lights being ignored, and residents not being changed. They were unable to do anything about it due to the shortage of staff. The gentleman still kept his job, and carried on with the same behaviors. The rooms in the building used to be hot during summer days with pee, and feces, and food stains embedded in the carpet throughout our hallways. The enclosed locked windows didn't help. The staff used to provide care dripping sweat leaning over me, or sometimes on my food. I would let them know they could turn my fan on for air circulation when they entered my room for their comfort. Although masks were required in all nursing home facilities at the time, I noticed that some staff members would occasionally enter my room without wearing one. Often providing questionable explanations for their lapse in protocol. Not realizing they were putting me at jeopardy of being exposed to a virus, or other sickness. Especially as I had a very weak immune, and respiratory system at this time in my recovery.

Safety precautions were not enforced always on a day-to-day basis in this nursing facility. Unless the state was coming in for an inspection. Even then, most facilities were aware when state inspectors were arriving. Then administration was able to tighten up the facility beforehand to avoid citations, or negative exposure to the facility. Though I was about four hours away from home, my support team would follow me. Visitations at the nursing homes in 2021 were changing due to COVID-19. My family would drive down from Columbus to see me at Edgewood Manor Of Lucasville Nursing Home in West Virginia. That after driving four hours. To have to stand outside of a window that was not opened in the extremely cold month of November. To look me in my eyes, and let me know everything was going to be ok. That he would support me, and be here for me throughout my healing journey. The visits would only last a half an hour. To then have to turn around, and drive another four hours back home. That meant a lot to me, and will be a memory that I will forever cherish.

Soon after, the government decided to open the doors for nursing homes to allow indoor personal visits with family, and friends. My support team would come to visit to discover the TV in my room was as big as a tablet. He immediately upgraded my TV to a bigger size. Also provided me with a fire stick to have more options with the TV selections. Being in West Virginia, most network stations wouldn't be available that I was interested in. I was beginning to wear clothes again. Things that were comfortable, and loose. Clothing helped me feel good about myself. I was starting over completely with everything. My support system would purchase nice items, and provide things according to the season.

My family was aware I didn't like the food so they would stock my dresser drawers with random things. Like cup of noodles, tuna packs, granola bars, trail mix, fruit cups. Which was perfect. I weighed roughly one hundred eighty pounds before my injury. Within two months of being paralyzed, my weight dropped significantly to one hundred forty-four pounds which was not normal for me, or healthy. I was now classified a fall risk even with the limited mobility. I had increased tone, muscle atrophy, a pressure sore on my upper buttocks; I was malnourished.

After doing my research in the area, I realized there were only two places that would deliver to this nursing home, due to its location. One of them was absolutely dissatisfying. Residents, and staff at the nursing home were wary of ordering from this particular company due to concerns about the food quality. The other was an Italian spot that was very well-known in the area for its exceptional food, and service. My family would order me lunch, and dinner from this restaurant my entire stay at Edgewood Manor Of Lucasville Nursing Home. It was not cheap, but worth it. Between all the pasta, pizza, and bread. Also, the other high-carb items on the menu helped me regain my body weight.

The nursing home would only be responsible for my breakfast. Which after meeting with my dietitian, we agreed on pancakes in the packet. Homemade french toast was served occasionally. Which was delicious when made by a specific individual in the kitchen. This nursing home was different. They would serve dishes like chili with peanut butter. This was a popular thing in West Virginia. Some of the other foods they would serve was unrecognizable, or in my opinion not edible. You would have to sometimes read the menu to know what you were looking at on the tray. I remember having meetings with the kitchen director who was really nice. She would explain to me on how they come up with their menu selections, and how they do things state-regulated. Also, she was willing to help accommodate me in any way to help get me to eat their food. Then I found out she would pack her lunch every day. She didn't even eat the food. I thought that was humorous.

Though my body was improving slowly, I was still at total assist. I needed help with feeding, my hygiene, bathing, dressing, and so much more. My occupational therapy, and physical therapy would now be working with me. Five times a week, daily for thirty minutes, each session. It wasn't much, but anything helped. We would work on bed mobility task. Static sitting for balance. I remember a particular moment when my therapists were working with me. They sat me on the edge of a raised mat table with one therapist in the front, and the other behind me for support. Then would instruct me to tighten my core if possible. Then let me try to remain sitting upright without falling over as they would let go. After trying this several times, and failing, I was able to accomplish thirty seconds staying upright by myself by not giving up. We were excited. This achievement was something monumental at this point of my recovery. It helped build my confidence; it was progress.

The omnicycle bike was an absolutely excellent aerobic exercise. My therapist would have to strap my feet in so they wouldn't fall off the pedals for safety. She also would H bandage my hands around the hand movement part of the machine for a full body workout to help support my grasp. I would be able to tolerate this particular machine for about fifteen minutes in a continuous workout in the beginning. Though the machine would help facilitate with most of the movements, I would still be able to see how much percentage of strength I was using on the digital screen display. Which was helpful so I could keep track of my improvements.

The electric standing machine, also known as sit to stand device would be next to try. It is a patient handling tool that helps people with limited mobility to stand up from a seated position. The device typically consists of a seat, backrest, and arm supports. The machine uses manual, or electric power to raise the user to a standing position. My occupational therapist, and physical therapist were both short, small framed women. As I did not have any leg strength, my body felt like dead weight, and they would need some extra assistance from fellow staff members after getting me fitted for the device. As I started to rise in a standing position in the machine, I was unable to see the exercise through. Due to the severe pain in my right shoulder from the ambulance driver mishandling me in the beginning of my recovery, the muscles in my chest, and shoulder were still healing. An unfortunate event was still affecting my rehab on certain activities which were noted by my therapist in my daily progress report. I still didn't give up; we attempted the exercise several times for several days. With consistent hard work, I was able to stand up between one to three minutes max at times. I would show signs of dizziness which is common in a spinal cord injury due to rapid changes of blood pressure, and fast movements. It was still an improvement.

Some other services my therapist provided me with was electrical muscle stimulation, and stretching. I thought both were beneficial due to the intense muscle spasms, and limited mobility. So between the Omni cycle which was important for blood circulation in muscle memory for my legs. The sitting up at the matt table which was effective for my trunk, core strength, and transfers. The electric standing machine with great attempts was still something to look forward to at a later date as I continued to heal. I felt like therapy was moving in the right direction. The feeding, dressing, and hygiene they assisted, and educated me on when they had extra time. Wheelchair assessments were required for the safety of the residents, and staff if you were operating an electric powered wheelchair within the facility. Therapy was very effective, and beneficial.

I was so thankful for the two very pleasant ladies who assisted me on my short journey at the nursing home. Going back to my first day when I arrived at this facility, I remember speaking to a few of the less confident staff members. Blatantly explaining that they rarely get a resident in my situation who has been paralyzed from the neck down who they had to care for who was with it mentally. It was uncharted territory for them. They weren't sure if they had all the right equipment, and experienced staff that I needed to help me on my healing journey.

Even though my case manager at my previous location highly recommended this facility to me, I would go on to explain to many of my caregivers that I was willing to guide them step by step with my care. The techniques, and safe suggestions I learned from my previous location. Shower days, I would remember how bad the smell was in the room. Just nasty grime, feces, and unnecessary things in the shower room that didn't belong. Though the nursing home had staff members responsible to maintain, and sanitize the shower rooms. Majority of the employees lacked enthusiasm to perform their duties. I used to dread shower days. Even though I expressed on many occasions about the cleanliness in many parts of the facility, I was ignored or not provided my day-to-day care needs. It was time for a change.

So I requested to have a care plan conference. This conference would include my family, the director of nursing, my case manager, my dietitian, and myself. We discussed various options like evaluating my current health state to see if it was fit to be able to relocate back home to family. Obviously, when the idea was presented a few times early in my recovery, it sounded good. Though ultimately, it would have been an irrational, unsafe decision on my end. Most importantly, a lot of pressure on my family, and friends. We also discussed how the building could make immediate changes to help make my stay feel more comfortable, and safe. Also, how we can work together to address all my medical needs accordingly to my progress, and care plan. I've come to realize a good care plan reflects my needs, and wishes. The plan will state who will do what, when, and how often, and it will be updated periodically to reflect changes in my needs. There were various ideas, solutions, and recommendations that we went over after an hour's meeting. Coming to an agreement with all participating members. I decided to stay for another two weeks to see if changes were going to be made. This particular time in healthcare dealing with nursing homes with the shortage of staff members. The individuals they would hire were questionable. While many staff members demonstrated genuine passion for their work, and a commitment to providing quality care, others seemed motivated solely by financial gain. However, nothing changed. Immediately, I took matters into my own hands.

I started researching nursing homes that were closer to the Massillon area, where I am from. Despite my case manager's tireless efforts, and supportive attitude, she consistently returned with unsuccessful placement options day after day. With a little research, I stumbled across a location that was only forty-five minutes away from Massillon. The facility is called Scenic Point Nursing Home & Rehabilitation, which is located in Millersburg Ohio. I reviewed the website online. Read over their mission statement for the facility. Then after looking at their pictures, and going over the reviews, I was sold. I presented this information to my caseworker; she then submitted the paperwork. I was approved. As I prepared to leave this location, I was surprised to find out that the act of packing up stirred a sense of emotional attachment, despite my overall dissatisfaction with the facility. This third destination marked another pivotal stop on my healing journey; I will always be grateful for the invaluable support, and guidance. Despite the brevity of my stay, 1 remained positive, and calm for safe travels to the next destination.

Scenic Point Nursing Home

11/25/2021 - 10/02/2023

Traveling through the mountains. Driving through the country scenery was so beautiful, peaceful, and calm. The trees, the smells, the noises, and animals. Everything about nature, and itself seemed so serene. As I reflect on my journey, I prepared to embark on the next phase of my path. I arrived. Greeted by a staff member who demonstrated remarkable professionalism, and politeness. Making a favorable first impression. After being checked in going through COVID-19 safety protocols to enter the facility, I was escorted to my room. Destination four, I was lucky enough to still not have a roommate throughout this whole recovery. Which I thought was safe, and beneficial in so many ways during this difficult time in the health care system.

After getting a few of my things settled in my room, my nurse performed a thorough assessment, checking my skin, body, and vital signs. Also giving me information on how my medications would be facilitated throughout the day. Since the beginning of my injury, I was always required to take a handful of medications. I would only take them one by one. A few of the nurses I came across in my recovery would get upset, or irritated. They didn't understand why I couldn't take them all at once like most of the other residents. I soon would be greeted by my case manager, who was full of energy, and passion for her job. Though she explained to me, I was her first resident on her caseload. I thought this was concerning because of the lack of experience, but unique because we could work together on this healing journey, and watch my story evolve into something special. She began her process with the normal sock, blue, bed routine to check my memory, and cognitive function. I've heard those words so many times from the three previous locations, I was able to repeat them backwards, and faster; we would laugh. She handed me my residents, and facility rights handbook. Then went over some paperwork that requested my signature. Plus informed me on a few other important subjects to help me with my stay at the nursing facility. That if I had any questions, she would always be available to assist. She was very helpful.

The nurses' assistants which were the staff that would handle the majority of my care on a day-to-day basis was a huge upgrade from my previous location. Most of the staff understood some of the responsibilities of caring for a quadriplegic. Though the facility was short-staffed, and my care would require more time for certain parts of the day. Especially being placed on a two-hour check-in change. Meaning a staff member is required to come and check on me every two hours to make sure that I was rotated in different positions to prevent pressure sores, or other complications with the recovery. Having a positive attitude, a likable personality, plus having knowledge, and standards about my own care, and recovery separated me from the other residents in the facility. I would see angry, or disrespectful, most importantly impatient residents making other staff members' job harder, and uncomfortable than it had to be. Which sometimes would affect the residents' day-to-day needs.

Over the course of my stay, I developed a strong bond with my care team, fostering a collaborative, and supportive environment that greatly contributed to my well-being. I was very aware of my surroundings. Men, and women lived at the nursing care facility here. All of us were here for a different reason. Some for rehabilitation short term stay at the facility. Though most of the residents could not take care of themselves physically, or mentally. Family members sent them here for better care, and a long-term or permanent stay at a facility. I noticed most of them were all equipped with a health care agent (also called a health care proxy, surrogate, or representative in some states) this is the person you name in your medical power of attorney (POA) to make health care decisions on your behalf. Though the court system has the authority to make that decision if you're ever unable to do so yourself. Also commonly known as a guardian, which is someone who oversees their healthcare needs in general. They're responsible for making sure the patient is provided proper care, maintenance, education, and support. Supply food, clothing, shelter, and necessaries. Authorize medical, surgical, dental, psychiatric, and psychological care (although some medical treatments, such as experimental treatments, require court approval).

Throughout my experience, I've learned having someone in control of your life has its pros, and cons for particular individuals. In the beginning of my stay at the nursing home, I was pressured to have a guardian to oversee my medical needs. I was not explained correctly what I would be signing over, but was requested to sign paperwork within a time frame. I was then thinking it was a good idea because I had a great support team. Not knowing how it would have affected me more badly in so many ways throughout my journey. After reviewing the information, and asking questions for several days, a concerned staff member stepped aside, and spoke with me about how this would be a bad decision. That I'm totally in my right mind, and aware of my care plan for a safe recovery. They were right; it was the best decision made for me. Though some of the higher-ups in the nursing facility did not agree.

I would soon discover the facility was majorly a psychiatric behavior place for men, and women. I would take my power wheelchair, and ride around the facility to look at the layout of the nursing home to see what it offered. To see the residents, the staff members. To realize I was truly grateful, and blessed after looking around. I could immediately notice the majority of the residents had their physical body intact, and working well, but did not have their mind intact. Some of the residents didn't have a clue what was going on. Some reasoning was the medications, or specific illnesses, and other various reasons. For me to have lost my body due to being paralyzed then still have my mind with a positive attitude, and a determined will to become a better version of myself was powerful. I knew nothing much about nursing homes or the healthcare system until I was placed in this situation. Being young at the age of thirty-four having a real-life insight experience on what's going on was challenging but rewarding.

I remember my first six months at least, I didn't even go outside. I didn't even speak to many of the staff members or the residents unless it was for a particular reason. I isolated myself to focus on my recovery. My mental health, and physical health. Also, many other key critical components that would benefit me along my recovery. I made sure I got rid of many distractions. I would focus on my daily habits, making sure things that I would want to get done, or plan were executed. Affirmations were big for me in so many ways. After building a few key relationships in the activities department, I was able to keep my room full of inspirational, and motivational decorations with creative quotes that would not only influence me, it was helpful, uplifting, plus meaningful for the staff members, and visitors who would come into my room. Especially due to specific parts of the building still being shut down due to COVID-19 to where a lot of my exercise activities were done in my room. I started to create a vibe. A space that was clean, and peaceful. Which would include books, crystals, waterfalls, air diffusers, plants. Inspiring, and motivating posters by influential people like Muhammad Ali, Bruce Lee, just a few to name. It was my space where work could be performed.

After a thorough evaluation by my therapist who was a female at the time, I had limited movement, and strength in both arms. I had limited movement, and strength, in both legs. Though at the time the left side of the body was showing improvements. I had full shoulder, and neck mobility with small signs of movement with my fingers. My body was progressing in healing, but still so far to overcome. My therapy sessions were forty-five minutes long, five days a week. Which would include the basic mom, and pops original workouts. Plus stretches that I thought were beneficial in so many ways. Though not enough for what I needed to get me to the next level. Especially with the shortage of time in days on my side. I knew without signs of physical improvement, I could be terminated from the therapy program. Most of the time, decisions like that were made by the insurance companies which controlled the whole market.

I was thankful, and blessed when I would find out that the administrator of Scenic Point Nursing Home signed off on my therapy each week. After the evaluation of my consistent progress notes from my therapist. That the building would cover the cost of my therapy. Considering most patients who were assigned to therapy, their workout sessions would likely only last between one to six weeks max. Then the patient would be released from the therapist's care plan. My therapy started on November 23 2021 which exceed successfully until August 7 of 2023. This was unheard of. I successfully completed four hundred thirty-three days of physical therapy at one location with no missed days, which was important. I understood early that a missed day documented on my paperwork could affect me negatively. Having a positive attitude, and a strong work ethic daily was important. No one wanted to work with someone who was angry, hateful, negative, or not willing to participate in activities that were instructed. I also came to realize that some therapeutic activities, such as stretching exercises, could have been just as effectively facilitated by family members, friends, or staff with available time, rather than requiring dedicated therapy sessions.

I wanted to utilize my forty-five minutes effectively, with more strenuous, and intense workouts that would challenge my mind, and body. So I requested a change in therapist. Instantly, I was placed under the care of the director of therapy department who reviewed, and jointly approved my referral to the facility. Which was perfect. Not only was he a male with a strong physical structure, he also had a great background of personal growth experiences, and achievements that would allow us to work together as a team. Most importantly, he had a great outlook on life, and a positive attitude. As of December 31, 2021, I began video recording my therapy sessions as a strategic means of self-monitoring, and progress tracking. This proactive approach enabled me to analyze my technique, pinpoint areas for improvement, and observe incremental advancements over the course of my therapy. I would start each workout video off with a powerful word like greatness. One of the first adjustments immediately made was we thought that I should start getting the body to stand up in an upright position as much as possible. The facility was equipped with a standing machine that would be beneficial to get the body in an upright position. To help promote better blood circulation, gut health, and allow me to enjoy other creative activities in a different position.

After a few sessions, we would begin to notice progress to where my therapist would allow me to sit at the edge of the bed. I would attempt to stand with his safety support, allowing me to use my own leg strength to support my own body weight. In the beginning, it was very difficult. It was a struggle, but progress was being made. After days of failure, days of not seeing the gains. The days of max help, and constant hard work, it all began to get recognized. Then rewarded with results. Which allowed me, and my therapist to quickly develop a covenant. A bond, a commitment to helping me regain my independence; we were a team. Growing up, I would always hear all it takes in life is for one person to believe in you. I found that guy, even though I believed in myself. I can honestly say throughout my recovery, there were only a few times he questioned my judgment. To realize my decisions weren't just based off of words, but how I felt internally. He respected, and understood early that I would always be honest with him about my body. I would frequently express to him how much I loved myself, and how important my health was to me. That I wouldn't jeopardize anything to hurt it. I was the only one who could explain what was going on inside my body throughout my recovery.

My mind is powerful. I was so in tune with what was going on in my recovery to where I could feel the healing of the nerves reconnecting. The muscles were gradually getting stronger, and growing, the blood flowing throughout the body. I was paying attention to the smallest things; it was something I didn't take for granted. I was able to give him results weekly, which sometimes were not always easy. I was always taking risks, or challenging myself to the next level safely. My positive mindset to continue to work toward my goals to be rewarded with healing in a short period became an obsession. We started incorporating other effective exercises to help improve my core strength, which would be beneficial in so many ways. Whether it was side to side movements, twisting, or back-and-forth movements. Anything to help with the stabilization of my body to help with balancing, and standing.

My stomach became a very serious commitment for me since the majority of my movements would benefit from stronger core muscles. My leg exercises were also a focal point at this time. Finally, the therapy room doors would open up for exercises after the COVID-19 pandemic. I carefully assessed the treatment room. It didn't have much. But what it did have, I knew if utilized correctly with my mindset, work ethic, and creativity, I would be able to figure something out to continue this recovery.

The first thing I noticed was an exercise bike; it was perfect. My therapist would take the seat off the bike to allow me to pull my electrical wheelchair up so that I could self pedal the bike for various exercises in time limits. At this time, I remember I was still in my electric wheelchair with a seatbelt. With leg straps to support me though I still had the leg strength, and movement to operate the exercise bike. This became an excellent additional activity I did five days a week, twenty to forty minutes a day. As I progressed, I was able to start self transferring from my wheelchair to the therapy bike assisted. Then unassisted on my own, which was a huge milestone.

The parallel bars were of great use as well. In the beginning, we attempted many times just trying to sit, to stand from my wheelchair to the parallel bars. The activities for the parallel bars were endless. From walking forward, to backwards, lateral movements, balancing activities, lunges, squats, step up in over activities. Pretty much anything to help me feel safe to successfully execute my exercises within the bars.

The platform walker was next. It was an excellent equipment to make me stand upright, but with wheels to allow me to walk. It had forearm rails to help assist a little bit with the upper body weight if needed as I attempted to take steps. May 24, 2022 at 10:34 am, I took my first steps. This was groundbreaking to my recovery. Words couldn't explain how my therapist, and I felt. The energy in the room was full of love, support, shock, and excitement. After a few attempts of the platform walker around the therapy room, I would then be allowed to utilize it in the hallways. Assisted with a therapist on both sides, and targets to meet to show progress as we worked diligently day after day. To gain a better gait in my walk, and better hip lift on my strides as I stepped forward, we would focus on the heel to toe strike on the ground to prevent dragging, and causing a trip and fall.

The platform walker also helped me gain better form, endurance, and strength within the muscles as I stood upright. It was a great exercise for getting the body back to walking normally again. The three-step stair platform was excellent for simulating steps in a small safe space. In the beginning, each leg had its pros, and cons. Whether it was one stepping up better than the other, or the other stepping down more confidently. Either way, the stairs were challenging especially trying to do reciprocal stepping up, and down the stairs. Which was not completed until I got on the stairs in the hallways at the exit, and entry points of the facility. The steps simulated real life situations; it was a full body workout. Handrails were always encouraged, and used for support, balance, and safety.

July 19, 2022 is a day to be remembered for me. To be given back the power to feed myself was a blessing. A person like myself who has OCD, or just plain out picky when it comes to eating, or who's doing the feeding. There were plenty of times when I had staff members cough, sneeze, breathe heavily, or talk over my food. Staff sometimes would take it upon themselves without asking to mix my mashed potatoes, and green beans, or meat. Just doing things the way they like to do them not asking if it's ok with me. So when I knew my wrist, and hands were ready to consistently execute the task without making too much of a mess. My first meal I fed myself was a chef salad. Something that I could poke with a fork, pick up, and put in my mouth successfully.

The same day, I decided it was time to discontinue my hoyer lift with my therapist's approval. That with noticeable improvements with my recovery, the care team, and I would perform self transfer from bed to wheelchair, or wheelchair to bed. In the beginning, we would use a gate belt, and a sliding board to help build confidence. To where nothing was needed, and I was self transferring on my own fairly quickly. The mat table in the therapy room was small. It didn't have a lift system; it was just stationary. We made it work after trying to simulate bed mobility exercises. Learning how to maneuver around on my own independently was huge. We would incorporate edge of the mat table exercises. One of my favorite exercises was always to set myself to the edge of the mat table, lower myself down to the ground completely as if I fell, and no one was at home to help me. I would be required after being down on my back, or stomach to get up safely on my hands, and knees. Then stand up, and have a seat safely back on the mat table, or my electric wheelchair. Though a lot of times in the beginning, failure was a part of the process. There was still gains physically, and mentally that allowed me after several attempts to gradually get better. To be able to execute the exercise on my own later on in my recovery.

August 16, 2022 was the day; being able to successfully brush my own teeth was a great feeling. Not having to wait on another individual to come, and help me in the mornings. Having their hand, or fingers in my mouth overly brushing, or too rough, or too soft, or gagging me. In the mornings, being able to get up, and self transfer to my wheelchair, and wheel over to my dresser to get my toothpaste, toothbrush, and go over to the sink to brush my own teeth was rewarding.

Following soon after August 26, 2022 was the first time I was able to have a bowel movement on the toilet. I felt like this sometimes is an activity that gets overlooked. To have to go to the bathroom on yourself, and required to call on someone else to change you. No privacy to the sacred parts on our body that we were born with was sometimes humiliating. I went through a time when the hangnails on my feet were reoccurring for months. They would cause extreme discomfort. The excess pus that would come out, or the swelling, and bleeding. I was scheduled to see a podiatrist. After examining my foot, my doctor came up with a solution to cut up the side of my toenails to alleviate the problem completely with no guarantees that the nail would grow back. The procedure did work on a few toes, but I had a total of eight hangnails. I revisited his office five times at least, until the problem was solved; it was a huge relief.

Though overall my health was improving day after day, I decided to get creative in the summertime. To attempt walking up, and down hills on the nursing home property with the approval, and assistance of my therapist. We set a date: April 13, 2023, it was a beautiful, sunny day. I began to prepare mentally for the challenges ahead. I was already anticipating the heat from the sun, the unevenness of the holes in the yard. The high grass, also gravity played an important role when I was walking down the hills which tested me. After several great attempts up, and down the hill. I would work hard until failure to where I lowered myself in the yard intentionally due to fatigue. Instead of quitting, or coming up with excuses. I decided to crawl to the finish line to be greeted, and surrounded with an absolutely amazing support team which included staff members from the nursing facility that helped along my journey. Supporting me on this activity was uplifting, inspiring, and motivational. Fueled with words of encouragement, cheers of joy, and good energy. Greatness was definitely displayed.

After strenuous activities, electrical muscle stimulation therapy was useful. I owned the wireless, and wired pads. The purpose of this equipment is to alleviate pain, reduce swelling, and improve the healing of injuries through increased blood flow to stimulate the muscle fibers in nerves, and target week muscles. Massaging the body, and stretching consistently were just as important. I was gifted a handheld massager which was perfect for when the facility was short staffed. Or if my outside resources were unavailable to come into the nursing home to assist. My support team purchased me two sets of finger-functioning robotic gloves from Amazon, which were convenient, and effective in helping build finger strengthening, and muscle memory connections to the mind so that the hands respond as the machine worked. My leg air heat compressors were relaxing. They helped with blood circulation, healing of the nerves, and muscle recovery.

Throughout my healing journey, I would accumulate a few random effective therapy devices, that would help aid my recovery which was gifted to me by family, friends, and staff members; I was very appreciative. One of my favorite gifts was the resistance bands, I still use to this day. One of the sets I could strap to the back of my door. The resistance bands were equipped for use of a variety of exercises that would help improve my strength, endurance, and mobility. The other set of resistance bands I used, and found beneficial was a secure waistband that was wrapped around my waist, and two others straps wrapped around both ankles. That way, you could safely attach the resistance bands to the hooks that were built in the straps, to attach to your waist, and ankles to do exercises like squats, lunges, or lateral movements. Though I was limited around the nursing facility with exercise equipment.

I would start to incorporate real life activities like cooking, cleaning, bed making, self dressing, self care. A lot of these activities were time-consuming, and utilized a lot of my energy. But with consistent attempts, it got easier. I would also do fun activities like shooting pool, playing basketball, chess, corn hole, and video games to help with hand coordination, and reaction.

I also got the opportunity to go swimming for the first time since my injury at a private resort. It was peaceful, and therapeutic. My first thought when my family asked if I wanted to go to the pool was to just tag along and set my body on the edge, and let my feet hang in the water. That changed when I got there. My confidence was beginning to build up to where I assessed the situation, and found a way to safely enter the water. To be able to sit down inside the pool on the edge because it had a built-in bench along the inside was a start. Then I would begin to stand up, balancing myself without falling over. Water is so powerful. My mind instantly went into workout mode to where my family, and I performed several exercises. After finishing up, I was able to successfully walk out of the pool into my wheelchair safely, with no help. This was a proud, and enjoyable moment.

Getting out of the nursing home facility to spend time with family, and friends was special, and much needed. Learning how to get back to being involved in the community with a temporary disability, and having to figure out new ways to move around independently went smoothly. Even if that was getting in, and out of vehicles, or going up, and down the stairs to get into houses. Even though I would have support to help a lot of the times. My pride, and mental focus to progress physically to do things on my own fueled me along during my healing journey. I would frustrate staff members, and most importantly my family members, and friends with one of my favorite sayings. Get off me. I got it. Get off me. I got it. Don't touch me. That meant leave me alone, and let me perform or do whatever I was doing. Some would laugh, and some would disagree, and get frustrated because all they wanted to do was help. For me, I felt a mindset like this was needed throughout my recovery. Especially after having to have someone take care of me twenty-four hours a day, not being able to care for myself was not a lifestyle that I wanted to get comfortable with. So when I would listen to my body as it progressed, and continue to heal. To where any given chance to do things on my own, I would take advantage of it.

The Canton McKinley Monument September 12, 2023 was a dream come true. An event that I envisioned at least six to eight months before it happened. Something that I was so delusional, and confident about that I knew if I set my mind to achieve it, it would happen. Exactly two years later, after being diagnosed of paralysis from the neck down, also my thirty sixth birthday, I successfully walked up ninety-seven steps with my walker. There were obstacles that tried to sabotage the event. The weather wasn't cooperating. It would start to rain. My cameraman was on a short time frame. My family was suggesting that I should reschedule. After a support team member, and I just drove an hour from Scenic Point Nursing Home to Canton, Ohio. To just turn around, and go back to just give up, or make excuses was not an option. With all this going on, I remained positive. I stuck with my plan to do what I set out to do, and that was walk the stairs. It was a great personal achievement.

Other obstacles I dealt with in my recovery was when I would try to transfer to an intensive rehabilitation center. Similar to the one I was at in the beginning of my recovery, now that I was recovering well, a lot of the facilities I would see were equipped with new state of the art equipment. They were staffed with an experienced, professional physical therapy team that I thought could help further my rehabilitation. I would be denied after several attempts of applying for different locations.

Though at times the facility, or therapy directors would approve my application, Insurance on the other hand would deny it for whatever reason. Being denied access to maybe what I thought could have been a better situation with my work ethic and mindset was frustrating. A few of the doctors, and insurance companies were trying to change my diagnosis from quadriplegic to muscle weakness. Yes, this sounds like a good thing. Yes, I was recovering considerably quickly at times. But clearly, if you work with me, or could see me in person, you would understand that I still needed assistance, and further therapy.

When I look back on it, it played out in my favor. A lot of the intensive therapy rehabilitation centers only allow short term residency stay at the facility, or provide outpatient therapy which usually ends between two to eight weeks, then you get sent home. Despite my efforts to excel, a lingering sense of resistance persisted. It seemed that the staff, and administration were divided in their support for my success. My experience within the healthcare system revealed a complex web of influences, where insurance interests, regulatory policies, and institutional protocols often intersected in ways that compromised the majority of the patients' care.

At Scenic Point Nursing Home, I perceived a lack of standardized protocols with policies, and procedures seemingly developed on an as-needed basis. This approach appeared to prioritize reputation, management, and the financial sustainability of the facility over other considerations. During my residency, I was privy to certain concerns, and inconsistencies expressed by staff members, and I personally witnessed incidents that raised questions about the facility's operations, and standards.

During my stay, I observed that personal issues among staff members sometimes carried over into their work, impacting the care, and attention provided to residents. Notably, this led to neglect, including delayed responses to call lights, inadequate personal care, and diminished social engagement. These lapses in care were troubling. As a resident, I formed connections with staff members who openly shared their personal, and professional challenges with me. My mental clarity, and attentive listening allowed me to gain insight into the facility's inner workings, revealing several concerning issues. Including inaccurate resident record-keeping, medication mismanagement, and loss. Misappropriation of company, and resident funds. Resident conflicts, and altercations. Also, the emotional impact of resident deaths. These experiences offered a distinctive perspective on the facility's operational challenges, and vulnerabilities.

I recall numerous instances where I'd share a pleasant conversation with a resident, only to wake up the next morning to the devastating news of their passing. However, my experiences were also scarred by a pervasive culture of dishonesty, negativity, and lack of communication among staff members. The disrespect exhibited by some staff toward their colleagues, and residents was awful. These issues occasionally created a toxic environment that hindered their ability to provide the best care possible. There were plenty of times when my personal rights were violated. I was instructed on several occasions by specific staff members, and residents to contact an ombudsman, which is a representative of the state who would advocate for me if my rights were being violated; I chose not to pursue.

My purpose for coming to this facility was for therapy services. To focus solely on my recovery, and get results, and I did. It was not to shine a bad light on the facility, the staff, or the healthcare system. On my door before you entered my room, I had a sign that read, let your next step be your best step. Meaning check your attitude, and energy before you enter. I encouraged positivity, an open mind, and teamwork in my presence. If I felt at any time that a staff member consistently didn't have my best interest, or just plain didn't want to do their job, I would ban them from my room immediately which was within my resident's rights. This would prohibit them from entering my room, or assisting with my care. Throughout my stay at the nursing home, my positivity, professionalism, hard work, and respect for the staff was overlooked many times, or frowned upon.

Most residents living at the nursing home were psychiatric patients; a lot of the employees over the years were used to verbal disrespect, unusual behaviors, and the lack of self-care for the residents. I was told many times that I wasn't their usual resident. I could clearly think for myself, and conduct my own care. Plus, I knew what was going on around me daily. During my residency at the nursing home, I engaged in consensual romantic relationships with certain staff members, which involved intimate activities both within, and outside the facility. Also, certain staff members permitted me to use vaping products containing THC, and nicotine within the facility, often providing them to me directly. Meanwhile allegations of staff misconduct, including substance use, and possession of narcotics, and alcohol on premises were frequently disregarded or unreported. This lack of accountability appeared to be linked to staffing shortages, inadequate oversight, or concerns about reputational damage.

Employees were always breaking the rules. Most importantly, there was no leadership in the building. You could always tell when state was coming into the nursing home facility. Usually then, all the higher-ups in the offices would be on the floors doing routine checks. Just helping out doing things that was out of character. I was fortunate enough to be provided a whole new wardrobe after having to start over due to the loss of previous belongings. I was gifted endless small affordable therapy devices that I could use to help during recovery due to the lack of equipment in the nursing home. I was able to be provided with top-notch personal hygiene, and care products.

Though I built a few relationships with individuals in the kitchen department, the food was dissatisfying, unhealthy, and cold most of the time. If I did find something suitable to eat, particular staff members would warm it up in the staff room microwave, which was forbidden for residents. The staff would order takeout food for me, also consistently fill my dresser drawers up with shelf life grocery store items. If I needed a little bit of money for miscellaneous things cash app was my best option, or just cash was given. I was extremely grateful, and blessed.

I would like to give a special thank you to my laundry keeper. During the beginning of my injury, for at least a year, I did not use any of the laundry service facilities for many different reasons. So, my family, friends, and staff members would take my laundry home weekly to clean. Until later on in my recovery, it became a burden. To where I met an amazing woman who decided to do my laundry personally. She was passionate about helping me out, and taking care of my belongings. Especially in nursing homes when things would come up missing, or get ruined from not getting handled properly, or mixed up in other resident's laundry. She was not only my laundry keeper, we became friends too. Her warm gentle smile, well soft-spoken voice, and positive attitude will always be remembered.

My housekeeper was full of energy; she took her job very seriously. Each room was cleaned thoroughly on her unit; all she needed was her music, and cleaning supplies. She was very easy to talk to. Very kind, and understood how I liked my room organized, cleaned, and smelling good. We developed a great friendship.

After suffering a life-threatening injury, I faced the daunting challenge of parenting from a nursing home. The abrupt transition from daily interactions with my children to prolonged separation was nothing short of devastating. For months, I was unable to see or speak to them. A mention of their names or a glimpse of their photos would trigger an intense emotional response. My nerve damage would react to these stimuli, causing my body to experience unexplainable, and unsettling sensations. These episodes were not only emotionally taxing but also potentially detrimental to my recovery. At times, it felt as though my body was on the verge of complete shutdown. The kids would come down, and visit occasionally on holidays like Thanksgiving, Father's Day, and one of their favorites, Easter. I remember stuffing, and hiding over eighty Easter eggs in my little room in the nursing home. For the kids, it wasn't so much the mystery of finding the eggs. It was a challenge to see who could get the most, the fastest. Let's not forget majority of them were full of candy, and money. Words can't explain how seeing them all together having fun, enjoying each other's company made me feel.

Despite facing numerous challenges, including poor treatment by some employees, and personal struggles, I came to realize that my experiences were transformative. The difficulties I encountered ultimately fostered mental growth, self-development, and resilience. As I navigated my healing journey, my positive attitude, strong work ethic, and determination emerged as invaluable assets. These qualities facilitated my personal growth but also inspired others, including staff members, residents, and family. Then it was time to relocate. Time to get back into the community, and utilize more resources. I was looking for a new start. I didn't have the finances, or credit to buy a house, and was not yet ready physically to live on my own.

I was then assigned a transitional coordinator. A person who would provide me with important information for community programs. Assist me with my new care plan, and advocate as we searched for my new relocation. We started to look into transitional living apartments where I would still get the home care, and therapy I needed to continue my successful recovery. My application was denied, after which I felt like my transitional coordinator lost hope. She struggled to find a suitable placement for me, citing my past as a barrier. However, I began to suspect that her inexperience and limited effort in addressing my unique situation were contributing factors.

I didn't lose hope. I just got involved more. I started doing research on my own, and asking questions. Shortly after, my fill-in case manager recommended the Joneses Residential Services located in Canton, Ohio. A group home located close to my hometown Massillon. After filling out the application for a place of residence, I was approved. I scheduled a day to look around the premises June 7, 2023. I did not discharge from Scenic Point Nursing Home until October 2, 2023. Discharging from a nursing home was not an easy process for me. It was time-consuming with the emails, phone calls, and paperwork was overwhelming. Especially having to wait on my approval for RSS, which is a residential state supplemental program that would help take care of a percentage of my rent due to my disability. While Social Security was responsible for paying the rest. I was required to have a scheduled date to see a primary care physician within two weeks of my discharge. I also had to set up a delivery service for my medications. Then order, and arrange pick up for medical supplies. Such as a shower chair, a walking rollator, and a few other miscellaneous items. Setting up community transportation was also essential. Home health care, and therapy services were challenging to acquire because I was transitioning to a group home. I observed that the transitional team faced challenges in providing optimal support for patients' community reentry. While I would wait to get my paperwork all approved, and submitted.

My transitional coordinator informed me of a program that would help me out with a funding balance of two thousand dollars to help get me back on my feet. I would shop strategically, and smart to find things that were affordable, and beneficial to my recovery, and livelihood. Throughout this process, I encountered numerous challenges, including gatekeepers who hindered my progress, individuals who failed to follow through on commitments, and service providers who seemed disinterested in performing their duties. These experiences took a significant emotional toll on me. I remained positive, and calm for safe travels to my next location.

DESTINATION FIVE
Jones Residential Services

10/02/2023 - To Current

Sixteen hundred dollars a month for my stay at the Jones Residential group home. This is what the state of Ohio requires each resident who wish to reside in a group home to pay. My Social Security income dispersed, a monthly funding of nine hundred forty-three dollars. RSS residential state services dispersed a monthly funding of eight hundred seventy-seven dollars, which equals one thousand eight hundred twenty dollars. This means, after I pay my landlord the sixteen hundred dollars for rent, I would be left over with a remaining balance of two hundred twenty dollars monthly allowance for myself. After I paid for my monthly cell phone bill, purchased a few hygiene self-care items, made a few small investments into Nalevate, my brand, there wasn't much left. Though those funds weren't dispersed immediately, until January 2024. I came home on October 2, 2023. Needless to say, I was behind on my rent for the first few months until the funding caught up. Waiting on funding from the Social Security office was always a slow process. My landlords were aware of the situation, and were patient because the money was guaranteed through the state. Though I was still living off of the thirty dollars a month funding which was what I was receiving from social security throughout my stay at the nursing home. I'm very thankful, and appreciative for my support team, family, friends, and staff members who stepped up in many ways time after time as they continued to support me along my healing journey.

Arriving at the Jones Residence, I noticed I would be living with four other individuals. The first thing I thought was sixteen hundred dollars apiece per resident equals eight thousand a month. Impressive for a black elderly couple that has achieved homeownership in this urban neighborhood. However, despite the peaceful atmosphere, the area lacks opportunities for families to prosper. My room is small, but ideal. I'm grateful. Not only did I outgrow the nursing home at this point in my recovery, it was perfect timing for a change of location, getting back into the community. Having a space that I could reset my mind for a new game plan. To continue on a safe recovery, and build my brand utilizing community resources that would benefit me on my road to success.

My transitional coordinator came through on my behalf. The two-thousand dollar waiver that I was approved for though it had restrictions on what it could be used for. Allowed me to shop for things within the budget to help get me off to a good start back into the community since I was starting over completely. I ordered a new bedroom set, safety equipment that would be functional, and safe to help me move along in the house, and a few other small miscellaneous things that I could use around me that were effective to help further aid along my progress in my recovery. My support team helped me with the painting, cleaning, cosmetic upgrades to the home. Getting things set up correctly for me was finally done after a week at least. I was settled in my room comfortably for me to move along as planned to set up my doctors' appointments, and therapy services.

Upon arrival to the group home, I was not established with a home healthcare provider, or therapy services. During my stay at Scenic Pointe Nursing Home, I didn't have much medical advice, guidance, or follow up appointments from previous doctors, or specialists until at the end of my stay in the nursing home. I had a saying I used to say. The help I didn't get, was all the help I needed. I researched then requested to be seen by a neurologist. A doctor that specializes in diagnosing, or treating patients that deal with nerve damage or pain. After meeting with the doctor a few times, I found him to be professional, kind, informative, and helpful. He would always listen to my concerns, and answer any of my questions with sound medical advice. Also, he made sure I was equipped with the necessary medications adjusted accordingly by dosage during my progress. Plus encouraged exercises that could be added to my daily routine. Procedures like botox to the areas not functioning properly due to muscle spasticity, or nerve damage was discussed. However, we decided to hold off because my body is still healing naturally well.

He would refer me to Cleveland Clinic Mercy Hospital therapy services, a branch that was located near me. I was so excited, and motivated to meet my new therapist, utilize different workout equipment, and continue to be challenged. Come to find out my insurance Medicaid only allowed me to have thirty visits for therapy per year. I moved back into the community on October 2, of 2023. I didn't get my therapy services started until November 28, 2023.

After working with the therapy scheduling department, I was able to secure, and take advantage of twelve effective therapy sessions ending on December 29, 2023 closing the calendar year. Then for my thirty official visits to start over in January 1, 2024. I would pick right up again on therapy services January 5, 2024 which would last until February 29, 2024. Physical therapy would only conclude with twelve official visits. My therapy sessions were scheduled three times a week then switched to two times a week forty-five minute sessions. It wasn't much, but beneficial. I worked with five different therapists who were professional, and had different exercising techniques, and ideas that could help aid along in my recovery. They also assisted me on new equipment such as the rowing machine, elliptical, and the treadmill equipped with harnesses for safety just to name a few. Soon to be terminated from the care of Cleveland Clinic Mercy Hospital to continue out my recovery on my own.

My evaluation physician thought that it might be a good idea to leave an additional fifteen days of therapy on the calendar year open for a later time in the year. That way if further complications, or if my body would decline, and need further assistance. I would still have days available to get the help I needed to get me back on track. Throughout my life, I never had interest, or established a social media account until I got injured. January 1, 2024, I uploaded my story on different platforms such as Facebook, Instagram, TikTok, and YouTube shorts. So that the videos I documented throughout my recovery could give others hope, and to find strength in their struggles. A visual of what took place during my healing journey. While doing so hopefully inspire, and motivate others.

Mid January, 2024, I would soon receive a phone call from a woman who is a friend of my landlord where I'm residing. She reviewed my content online, and saw the event I performed on September 12, 2023 on my birthday. When I walked up the Canton McKinley Monument the first time for my two-year anniversary for my recovery. She went on to explain to me that her New Year's resolution was to make healthier lifestyle choices by working out, and that she would like to walk the Canton McKinley Monument stairs, but with me. Words couldn't explain how she made me feel at that moment. So I immediately started planning an event, something bigger than just two, or three people walking up the stairs. I wanted to get the community involved, family, and friends involved to give them an experience to remember.

February 10, 2024 will always be a day to look back on. The event was a success. My message was we all start together. We finish together. We all finish first place. I want to personally give a special thanks to the Canton, Ohio fire department that attended, and to all the amazing individuals who came, supported, and participated. Continuing this recovery has given me pure joy. Now I would decide to take some time off physically from the workouts, and would focus on other adventures, since my release from the nursing home. I was able to organize, and conquer many inspiring, impactful community events.

Trademarking Nalevate was a huge personal accomplishment. In addition, I created an LLC for Nalevate which I'm sure will be beneficial for me along my journey. I've developed a clothing line called Nalevate Inspirational Apparel Company. Starting a nonprofit for Nalevate foundations will be coming soon. As well as motivational speaking, podcasting, interviews, and documentaries will become available. Most importantly, I'm building valuable, and important relationships with all the right people to help achieve my goals. I've also been participating in virtual seminars, and webinars to acquire more knowledge.

March 1, 2024, is when I began my first day of writing this book. A piece of work that I could tell my story, and deliver a message that would be inspiring, and motivating to others. I would like this book to be also informative for those who know that someday we may have a family member, friend, or children, even ourselves, placed in a nursing home, hospital facility, transitional living, or group home due to whatever trauma or reason. My mission is to understand everybody has a story. An individual isn't going to let your story triumph their story. The only difference is how we overcome them. So knowing this, listening, and being observant of body language, and the mind of individuals has been my best virtual memory. In life, trauma, adversity, challenges, and failure are all a part of the journey. So if hearing my story on how I believed in myself, stayed true to my identity, envisioned a plan, and executed the process to produce results, can help inspire, and motivate to transform a person to be a better version of one's self, then I have achieved greatness.

Before my release from Scenic Point Nursing Home, I was able to create a word. Nalevate. I classified it as a verb, a word that demands action. The definition of Nalevate. To overcome adversity, and challenges. Transition, and grow mentally to be the best version of oneself. When I created this word, I thought of something representing me. Looking around today in the world, Nalevate represents us. We all go through some sort of adversity, and challenges of some sort; it's how we overcome them.

While residing at Scenic Point Nursing Home, I've had my fair share of adversity, and challenges. September 1, 2023, I lost my brother. Reginald McCullough, you will be forever loved , and remembered. I would like to personally dedicate my book to you. My brother throughout my journey I've learned through trauma there's healing, and with the right mindset, anything is possible. When I found out about my brother's passing, I prepared a speech that I would like to share. This is a serious moment for me. And what makes this moment serious for me is that I'm sitting in a room amongst family, and friends. And disguised in human form are some enemies. We're all aware our family is broken. It's unfortunate. Because looking around, all I can see is beauty, wisdom, strength, and love. But on the flip side, I can see pain, selfishness, negativity, and most importantly regret. Sometimes, we don't appreciate the good things until we lose them. Sometimes we don't value the people we have in our lives, till we lose them. Sometimes we don't appreciate a nice house. A nice job, a good mother or father, a sister or brother, and so forth. Until we lose them. We throw people away so easily. Sometimes, we're going to have to sit, and understand what we're throwing away today, we might need tomorrow. I feel like we threw Reggie away before his passing, and I'm guilty of that. I'm sorry Reg. Mental illness is real, depression, loneliness, lack of self-love is at an all-time high. I'm not saying any of us could have saved him. But an overdose. Maybe that could have been prevented if his heart was full of our love, and support, and positive energy from his family, and friends. We will never know.

We're living in a time with disruption, distraction, hate, fear, gossip, and most importantly, negativity is being accepted. Because we're comfortable being uncomfortable because it's all we know. So, with all this being said, I'm asking all to consider a personal transformation. To become a better version of ourselves every day. One moment at a time. We all have the ability to just do the right things by yourself, and others. Reggie doesn't have this option, we do. So I'm here today to provide us with hope, a sense of inspiration, and motivation. I'm not only sad today, but grateful my words can activate this greatness I know we all have in us. Knowing my words can fuel your thoughts for the rest of your day, and life. It's time to heal. I love you Reg. Thank you! I will remain positive, and calm for safe travels to my next location.

ACKNOWLEDGMENTS

As I reflect on my transformative journey, I am reminded of the countless individuals who have played a pivotal role in my recovery, and growth. It is with heartfelt gratitude that I acknowledge the following people:

Medical Professionals

To Dr. Rishi Goel, Aultman Neuro Surgeon, I extend my deepest appreciation for your exceptional care, and expertise. Your dedication to your patients is truly inspiring.

Support Network

To my loving family, and friends, I thank you for your unwavering support, encouragement, and love. Your presence in my life has been a constant source of strength, and motivation.

Healthcare Team

I would like to express my gratitude to the entire healthcare team that cared for me during my recovery, including administrators, doctors, case managers, nurses, STNA's, therapists, and activities department staff. Your collective efforts have made a profound impact on my life.

Unsung Heroes

To the laundry workers, janitors, maintenance department staff, and food services employees, I appreciate your tireless efforts to ensure my comfort, and well-being during my stay.

Transitional Support

Thank you to my transitional coordinators, and landlords, who helped facilitate my transition back into the community.

Strangers Turned Angels

To the strangers I met along the way, who offered words of encouragement, support, and kindness, I am eternally grateful. You have reminded me that humanity is full of compassion, and love.

This journey has taught me that overcoming adversity is not a solitary endeavor. It takes a village of supportive individuals who believe in our potential. I am honored to have had such an incredible team behind me.

Thank you.
Lanale Robinson

AUTHOR BIOGRAPHY

Lanale Robinson is a devoted father of three, author, and motivational speaker. Born and raised in Massillon, Ohio, Lanale developed a passion for sports, and construction at a young age. However, his life took a dramatic turn in 2021 when he was paralyzed from the neck down. Diagnosed with quadriplegia, Lanale has made remarkable progress, relearning to  walk, and regaining independence. Through his journey, he created the concept of "Nalevate" and wrote his debut book to inspire, and empower others to find strength in their struggles. To learn more, purchase his book, or explore Nalevate Inspirational Apparel Company. Visit nalevate.net

www.ingramcontent.com/pod-product-compliance
Lightning Source LLC
Chambersburg PA
CBHW051235120626

46547CB00013B/1661